Exercise Addiction: When Fitness Becomes an Obsession

Exercise Addiction:

When Fitness Becomes an Obsession

Laura Kaminker

THE ROSEN PUBLISHING GROUP, INC.
NEW YORK

For Karen, Marah, and Joy.

Acknowledgments:
The author thanks the young women who shared their stories with her. She also wishes to acknowledge the many nutritionists and therapists whose knowledge and dedication help people overcome eating disorders. Special thanks to Sondra Kronberg of the Eating Disorder Council of Long Island, New York.

The people pictured in this book are only models. They in no way practice or endorse the activities illustrated. Captions serve only to explain the subjects of photographs and do not in any way imply a connection between the real-life models and the staged situations. News agency photos are exceptions.

Published in 1998 by The Rosen Publishing Group, Inc.
29 East 21st Street, New York, NY 10010

Library of Congress Cataloging-in-Publication Data

Kaminker, Laura.
Exercise addiction: when fitness becomes an obsession / Laura Kaminker — 1st ed.
          p.   cm. — (The teen health library of eating disorder prevention)
Includes index.
Summary: Focuses on exercise addiction and its relationship to eating disorders; explains how compulsive exercise can be harmful and how one can get help to deal with it.
ISBN 0-8239-2759-8
1. Exercise addiction—Juvenile literature. 2. Eating disorders—Juvenile literature. [1. Exercise addiction. 2. Eating disorders.] I. Title. II. Series.
RC569.5.E94K36 1998
616.86—dc21   97-48832
                                                                                      CIP
                                                                                       AC

Manufactured in the United States of America

Contents

Introduction

Stacy gently closes the door behind her and tiptoes up the stairs. She hurries to her room so that no one will see her sweaty running clothes. Stacy isn't allowed to run at night, because her parents think it's unsafe. Tonight she told them she was studying at a friend's house. In her room, Stacy stands in front of the mirror, sideways, looking at her stomach, her thighs, her behind. Her running shorts and T-shirt are soaked with perspiration. Tonight she ran farther than ever. She thinks, I should have gone farther.

In her mind, Stacy hears her friends' voices. "You have so much discipline! You're so focused. I wish I could be like you."

Why would anyone want to be like me? Stacy wonders. At lunch today, the same friends were teasing her about how little she eats. "I've never seen Stacy eat anything with fat in it." "I've never seen her eat one cookie or one piece of candy." They were all laughing and joking. To prove them wrong, Stacy ate a handful of her friend's M&Ms. Now, thinking of those candies, Stacy does 100 crunches, her second set that day.

After her shower, Stacy says good night to her parents. Her mother asks, "Did you get a lot done?" and Stacy lies about the schoolwork she supposedly did at her friend's house. Stacy's parents don't know how much she works out. They don't know that she thinks about her body all day, every day. *I can never tell them,* she thinks. *They would think I'm crazy.*

When Jacki's mother and stepfather were splitting up, Jacki couldn't tell anyone how bad she felt. As the oldest child, everyone counted on her to be strong for her brothers and sisters. She wanted to talk to her father, but he was too busy with his new wife. At school, Jacki still got all As, played volleyball, and belonged to the drama club. But life at home got worse and worse. Her mother and stepfather argued all the time. Then arguing turned to screaming, and screaming turned to hitting. Her mother didn't seem to notice her anymore. Jacki just wanted to disappear. Going to the gym was a good escape. While she was in aerobics class or climbing on the Stairmaster, Jacki didn't think about her problems.

When Jacki started to lose weight, she felt a little better. There was something satisfying about knowing she could do it—and she was very good at it. First she stopped drinking soda and eating candy and chips.

Then she stopped eating meat. She started counting exactly how many calories she consumed each day. At the same time, she would count how many calories she burned from exercising. The list of foods she didn't eat grew longer and longer. When she couldn't eat any less, Jacki started making herself throw up.

She began to weigh herself more frequently—first every day, then a few times a day, then every chance she could. Every day became a challenge—to try to exercise a little more, to eat a little less. If she lost half a pound, it was a good day. If the number on the scale stayed the same or went up, she would exercise more.

Soon Jacki's life revolved around her exercise routine. She would wake up at 4:00 AM and exercise for three hours before school. After school, she would do her homework as quickly as possible, then go to the gym for two hours, then come home and do 500 sit-ups. Jacki quit the volleyball team and the drama club, and she lost touch with all her friends—but she didn't care. Jackie had no time for friends. She only had time for exercise.

A year later, Jacki had to leave school. She was too weak to walk to her classes. Her arms and legs were as thin as toothpicks. Her hair, which had been thick and shiny, was falling out in clumps. She cried herself to sleep every night. When Jacki first went to the Eating Disorders Clinic, she thought they might turn her away because she was too heavy. She weighed seventy-six pounds.

Many people connect their worth as people with the numbers they see on a scale. This belief contributes greatly to a negative body image.

Experts estimate that more than 8 million Americans suffer from eating disorders. Ninety to 95 percent are women. For many, the problem begins when they are teenagers. An eating disorder is a complicated psychological, emotional, and physical problem. Cultural influences can also contribute to an eating disorder. Women experience a lot of pressure from society to be thin and attractive. Some believe this is the reason more women suffer from eating disorders than men. Still, the number of males with eating disorders is increasing.

People with eating disorders are terrified of gaining weight. They are extremely concerned with the size and shape of their bodies. They think they are too heavy and need to lose weight, even though they are at or below a healthy weight. Because of this, they eat and exercise in unhealthy ways.

If it becomes severe, an eating disorder can take over a person's life. Unless that person gets help—and wants help—that person may die. According to Anorexia Nervosa and Related Eating Disorders, Inc. (ANRED), 20 percent of people with a serious eating disorder die if they don't get treatment.

The two main eating disorders are anorexia nervosa and bulimia nervosa. Compulsive eating (also referred to as binge eating disorder) is also a serious problem. Compulsive exercise is currently classified as a related eating disorder problem, and many experts believe the number of people suffering from it is growing. Compulsive exercise is also called exercise bulimia or exercise addiction.

Each of these disorders is a different type of behavior, but most people with eating disorders suffer from symptoms that fall into more than one category. In other words, many people have symptoms of anorexia and bulimia, or bulimia and exercise bulimia, or any combination of the four disorders.

This book is about eating disorders, specifically exercise addiction. It explains what an eating disorder is, why people have them, and how they are harmful. The book also explains the difference between healthy exercise and compulsive exercise, why people become addicted to exercise, how it can hurt you, and how to get help.

This book is also for everyone who worries about weight, who talks about dieting, who counts calories, and who wishes to be thinner. If you feel worried or depressed when you miss a day of exercise, this book is for you. And if you've ever wondered whether you have a problem with eating and exercise, this book is especially for you.

What Is an Eating Disorder?

"If I feel full after I eat, I think I've gained weight. I look in the mirror, and if I can't see the muscles in my stomach, I make myself throw up."

"During my senior year in high school, the girls started talking about 'the freshman fifteen'—the weight they say everyone gains during their first year of college. I was so afraid that would happen to me. The summer after graduation, we all joined a gym together. But I was the only one who went every day. First I'd take the aerobics class, then

I'd decide to stay for the weight-training class afterward, and before I knew it, three hours had gone by. Then I started canceling things so I could go running at night. My mom hated me running late at night, but it was the only time I could go, so I'd sneak out of the house. If I missed one day, I was convinced I had gained ten pounds."

"At a red light, I contract my abs. Waiting at the bank, I do toe stands to work my calves. I work out every morning and every night. After my workout, while I'm watching TV, I do lunges and bicep curls. I can't sit still because I'm afraid I'll gain weight."

People with eating disorders are preoccupied with the size and shape of their bodies. Because they judge themselves according to how much they weigh and what their bodies look like, they are terrified of gaining weight. To them, gaining weight is a failure and losing weight equals success. Their self-images become distorted, so they believe they are fat or flabby, even though they are not.

Anorexia Nervosa

The best-known eating disorder is probably anorexia nervosa (usually called anorexia). People suffering from anorexia starve themselves in order to lose weight. The condition usually begins gradually.

13

It's difficult to remember that we should not judge ourselves or others based on what we look like.

They will make certain foods off limits, and will eat only specific amounts of food. As time goes on, the list of foods they permit themselves to eat grows shorter. This is called restricted eating. People with anorexia will also fast, which means they will go for long periods of time without eating. Eventually they lose dangerous, unhealthy amounts of weight.

Bulimia Nervosa

People suffering from bulimia nervosa (usually called bulimia) make themselves vomit in order to get rid of what they have eaten. They may also use drugs that cause vomiting or diarrhea—anything to get the food out of their bodies. This behavior is called purging. Some people with bulimia starve themselves, then throw up what little they do eat. Others eat huge amounts of food—called bingeing—then make themselves vomit. This cycle is often called binge and purge.

Compulsive Eating

People with compulsive eating disorder (also called binge eating disorder) eat large amounts of food but don't purge it from their bodies. Everyone overeats occasionally, but people with compulsive eating disorder do it frequently. They eat huge amounts of food very quickly whether or not they feel hungry. They usually do this in private. They feel unable to control what or how much they eat. Afterward, they feel depressed, guilty, and disgusted with themselves. Compulsive eating is different from the other eating disorders, because the person is not trying to lose weight.

Compulsive Exercise

Compulsive exercise is characterized by using exercise to get rid of calories. This behavior is also known as exercise bulimia because the person is using exercise to purge calories from his or her system. The compulsive exerciser might also eat compulsively, restrict food intake, throw up, and/or take laxatives, diet pills, or other drugs, or any combination of these.

Compulsive exercise is also a bit different from other eating disorders: it can be a lot easier to hide. If a person stops eating, his or her parents and friends will probably become worried. But since exercise is usually a positive, worthwhile activity, people who stick to an exercise routine are often praised for their discipline. The behavior that wins compliments may actually

When people exercise only because they want to get rid of calories, they are in danger of becoming compulsive exercisers. Exercise should be just one of many aspects of our lives.

be harmful. When exercise takes over your life, when it isolates you, when it becomes the sole focus of your thoughts, then it has become unhealthy.

If you are struggling with compulsive exercise or any other eating disorder, remember that you are not alone. Millions of Americans suffer from eating disorders. Many others deal with eating and exercise problems that may not be severe enough to be called eating disorders but still put them at risk.

One reason for this is our culture's emphasis on physical appearance. Too often, people are judged by how they look, rather than who they are. In movies, magazines, and on TV, happy, successful, beautiful people are young and thin, while overweight people are often portrayed negatively. If you were to believe what you see in the media, you might think everyone in the world was thin. But people come in all shapes and sizes.

The Ideal

Young men and women are bombarded with images of what their bodies are supposed to look like. These images project a body shape that is considered the ideal shape, but it's not a reality. Very few men and women actually look like the ideal, and trying to reach that ideal is dangerous and unhealthy for most people. When we measure ourselves against these images, we can feel inadequate, no matter what we look like. Advertising relies on and targets this feeling of inadequacy to sell us products that supposedly improve our appearance.

What is considered the ideal body shape varies from culture to culture and is different at different times. One hundred years ago, a pale and round appearance was considered healthy and attractive because it meant that a person lived well and did not have to work outdoors. Being thin and tan was considered unattractive because this meant a person had limited resources.

Each of us has our own natural body type. Just as people differ in height and hair color, they differ in body shape and size. But because everywhere we look we see an ideal for women that is very thin and an ideal for men that is slim and muscular, many men and women think they need to drastically change their bodies.

Growing Up

Puberty is the time when girls become women and boys become men. During puberty, it is normal for females to gain weight. This is part of the natural process of becoming a healthy, adult woman. Unfortunately, many girls are unprepared for these physical changes. All around them are images of very thin women, advertisements for exercise equipment and diet shakes, and magazine articles about how to lose weight. They believe this natural, healthy weight gain is bad, and they begin to diet.

Exercise Enters the Picture

Since the 1980s, our society has become more aware of the connection between exercise and good health. At the same time, there has also been more of an emphasis on using exercise to change and improve our appearance. Take a look in your favorite magazine. Is there an article about exercise? What does it say? Does it emphasize health benefits, like preventing heart disease and strengthening bones? Does it talk about how and why exercise makes you feel good inside? Or is it about how to get a flat stomach and firm thighs, or how to lose weight? Experts believe that the emphasis on exercise as a weight-loss tool is causing a sharp increase in the number of people who exercise compulsively.

"Ab Roller! New Health Rider! Thighmaster Plus! Every time I turn on the TV I see ads for exercise equipment. The other day I saw a commercial for a treadmill. They showed pictures of a gooey dessert. A voice says, 'This isn't a hot-fudge sundae, it's an hour on the treadmill.' That is a commercial for exercise bulimia."

Because exercise is considered admirable and healthy, compulsive exercise is easy to hide. If you told your best friend that you threw up after every meal, your friend might be shocked or upset. But if you told your friend you exercised every day, he or she would admire you for your discipline and commitment. You can see how exercise can become an easily hidden addiction.

There's nothing wrong with wanting to look good. But when you feel that being thin is the most important thing in your life, and you believe that gaining weight is the most awful thing that could happen to you, then it is time to reexamine your priorities.

Some common signs of eating disorders are:

- Constantly thinking about the size and shape of your body
- Constantly thinking about how much you weigh and weighing yourself repeatedly
- Constantly thinking about food, cooking, and eating
- Eating only certain foods in specific and limited amounts
- Keeping a list of what foods are okay to eat
- Wanting to eat alone, feeling uncomfortable eating with other people
- Not feeling good about yourself unless you are thin—but never being satisfied with how thin you are
- Feeling that you should be exercising

more—no matter how much you
exercise
- ❑ Feeling competitive about dieting,
wanting to be the thinnest or the
smallest
- ❑ Taking diet pills or laxatives
- ❑ Continuing to diet, even after you are
thin
- ❑ Purposely losing lots of weight very
quickly
- ❑ Forcing yourself to throw up
- ❑ No longer having your period

If anything on this list describes you, you may
have an eating disorder. You can contact one or
more of the organizations listed at the end of this
book for further information and help.

You don't have to have every symptom on the list
to have an eating disorder. If some of them sound
familiar to you, read on.

When Does Exercise Become Compulsive Exercise?

"I exercised a minimum of three hours a day, at least six days a week, sometimes seven. At my worst, I was going six to seven hours a day. I belonged to two different gyms. They both had limits on how long I could stay to work out. So when they would kick me out of one gym, I would just go to the other one."

"I gave up my whole social life. If I had the choice between going out with my friends and going to the gym, I'd go to the gym. At the time I didn't see anything wrong with it. Now I look back and say, Oh my gosh, I missed so much. But back then I didn't care. I was terrified of getting bigger, so I had to keep going."

Exercise is an important part of staying healthy. The

Centers for Disease Control and Prevention, a government agency that studies many health issues, including how nutrition and exercise affect our health, has proven that exercise reduces the risk of high blood pressure and heart disease, which kill thousands of Americans every year. Girls and women who exercise lessen their odds of getting breast cancer and osteoporosis, a disease that causes bones to weaken and break.

A few years ago, the Women's Sports Foundation compared girls who engage in sports and girls who don't. The study found that the girls who participated in some form of aerobic exercise—any activity that gets your heart pumping and your lungs working hard—were happier, did better in school, and had higher self-esteem than the girls who didn't. Other research studies have yielded similar results.

Exercise has a positive effect on happiness and self-esteem for several reasons. When our bodies are more physically fit, more oxygen gets to the brain and the heart. Our muscles are stronger and firmer. Also our metabolism is higher, which means that more of the food we eat turns to energy and less turns to fat. Exercise may also strengthen the immune system, the body's defense system against disease and infection. All of these things make us healthier, and being healthier can make us feel more confident. And, as anyone who has ever gone for a

Healthy exercise has many benefits. It makes people feel good and gives them confidence to take on new challenges.

run or worked out at a gym when they were upset or angry knows, exercise relieves stress. Many people find that when they exercise regularly, they sleep better, have more energy, and are less likely to feel depressed.

In addition to the physical benefits of exercise, playing sports, especially team sports, can have psychological benefits. When we play sports, we learn to be more assertive, to compete, and to work as a team. These skills are part of having healthy self-esteem.

So What's the Catch?

But just because exercise is healthy, it doesn't mean that more exercise is even healthier. It is possible to exercise too much and for the wrong reasons. Some people become addicted to exercise. This addiction is called compulsive exercise. When people become addicted to exercise, they no longer get its positive benefits. Instead, their exercise is unhealthy. And, like an addiction to alcohol, cocaine, or any other drug, an addiction to exercise can destroy your life.

People who exercise compulsively feel that they must work out—not because they want to but because they have to. They use exercise as a way to purge calories from their bodies.

"I started sneaking out of the house to run, or I'd run when my parents weren't home, so they wouldn't know how often I went. I'm in an all-honors program at school and I play two instruments that I have to practice. When it got too hard to fit in the running, I started getting up early in the morning. Before long I was up at four every morning so that I could run seven or eight miles. Then I started running after school, too, so I could get in more miles. I tried to eat as little as possible,

and I made myself run an extra mile for every hundred calories I ate. Pretty soon I was up to sixty miles a week. Every day after I ran, I'd put my school uniform back on so my mom wouldn't suspect anything. During the summer, I worked two different jobs, but managed to get in about eighty-five to ninety miles a week. Now it's fall, and I'm up to about 100 miles a week."

People often start exercising because they want to lose weight. Or they may be going through a difficult time in their lives, and exercise helps relieve the tension. But if their self-image gets connected to their ability to exercise, they begin to base their value as human beings on how much they work out.

Discipline or Danger?

Exercise becomes compulsive when people feel worthless and guilty if they don't exercise. In order to feel good about themselves, they must work out every day. Anyone who exercises regularly has discipline and commitment. But there's a difference between having a commitment to your exercise routine and being excessively rigid about it. Healthy exercisers are committed to exercise, but if they have to skip a few days or weeks or change their routine, they make the adjustment without having a bad day or thinking they're worthless. If compulsive exercisers are forced to change or stop their

When someone becomes depressed because he or she has missed a workout, it is a warning sign of compulsive exercise disorder.

exercise routine for any reason, they become angry, depressed, or stressed out. That is why they will run even if the weather makes it dangerous to do so. They will take an aerobics class with a torn muscle. If their friends are going to the beach at a time when they usually exercise, they'll make up excuses and go to the gym. To compulsive exercisers, exercise is much more important than a social life.

"Sometimes I stay home 'sick' so I can run for most of the day. Running has become my life. I run until I'm so tired that my whole body is numb to everything around me. It's taken the place of my obsession with food. I'm scared to death to stop."

Compulsive exercisers think that they must exercise every single day in order to stay the same shape and size. If they are forced to miss one workout, they imagine that their muscles have become soft or that they've gained weight. They never feel satisfied with how their bodies look.

"I exercise three times a day. When I'm not exercising, I'm thinking about exercise. I exercise until I practically can't walk. Now I'm starting to skip meals, too. All I want is to be skinny."

This checklist can help you tell if your healthy exercise routine is becoming compulsive. If you check off any of these statements, you're probably exercising for the wrong reasons. If you check off three or more statements, please consider getting help.

- ❑ I force myself to exercise even if I don't feel well or I'm injured.
- ❑ I become depressed or upset if I miss a workout.
- ❑ I figure out how much to exercise based on how much I ate. If I eat more, I exercise more.
- ❑ I lie to my friends and turn down dates or invitations from friends and family rather than change my exercise routine.

- I have good days or bad days according to whether or not I've exercised.
- I have trouble sitting still because I think I'm not burning calories.
- If I don't exercise one day, I think I've gotten bigger or my muscles have gotten soft.
- Friends and family complain that I exercise too much.
- I've had to drop activities to fit in more exercise.
- I sometimes lie about how much or how often I exercise.

It's important to remember that even the most extreme eating disorder usually begins as a mild one. It can be very difficult for someone with an eating disorder to admit—especially to themselves—that they have a problem. If you suspect you have an eating disorder, please consider speaking to someone about it. Tell someone you trust—a teacher, a relative, your best friend—that you are concerned. Or go to a counseling center and talk to a counselor. You are not alone, and you can get help.

Why Do People Develop Eating Disorders?

There is no easy answer to why people develop eating disorders. Eating disorders are complex problems. They are caused by a combination of many factors—psychological issues, biological issues, family influences, and messages from society. Also, there is often a "trigger"—a disturbing event in a person's life that he or she responds to with excessive diet and/or exercise.

Most eating disorders have several causes, but the person with an eating disorder is not aware of them. The people quoted in this chapter have all recovered from eating disorders. They are sharing insights they have gained since recovering.

Let's look at some of the causes of eating disorders.

Psychological Factors

"If I didn't exercise, I felt worthless, like a total failure."

"I thought all of the bad things that had happened in my life were my fault. I didn't know it at the time, but I was punishing myself—by starving myself and making myself throw up."

"I had to be the best at everything I did. If there was a test, I had to get the highest grade. If girls were going to diet, I had to be the thinnest."

"When I binged and then exercised, I felt strong and powerful."

"On the outside, I was the perfect little girl. Inside, I was angry at my parents. But perfect little girls can't get angry. So I turned all the anger against myself."

A large part of eating disorders is psychological. People who suffer from eating disorders tend to be perfectionists. No matter what they do—get excellent grades, have many talents and abilities, have a full social calendar—they still feel inadequate. Perfection is an unrealistic goal.

People with eating disorders may get angry and upset, but they don't feel safe or know how to express their feelings. They are very concerned with pleasing people and being liked. They're afraid that if they show anger, people won't like them.

Family Factors

"My mother was too busy with her own problems to pay much attention to me. I was expected to just get on with my life by myself. When I weighed eighty pounds, I finally got her attention."

"I wasn't allowed to make any decisions for myself. I thought, If I can't be trusted to make one little decision, I must be a total loser. My weight was the one area of my life that I had control over. No one could make me eat if I didn't want to."

"I didn't realize it at the time, but I was also punishing my parents. They wanted me to eat, so I wouldn't eat. I wanted to hurt them, because they had hurt me."

"An eating disorder is a way of numbing out. You're too busy planning what you're going to eat, throwing up,

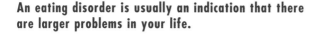

An eating disorder is usually an indication that there are larger problems in your life.

exercising, arranging the food on your plate, and counting calories to feel your own pain. After a while, you're too hungry, dizzy, nauseous, and weak to feel much of anything."

People with eating disorders tend to have family problems. Their home lives are often unstable or full of disruptions, such as a parent who gets divorced and remarried, or a family that moves from city to city. The eating disorder becomes a way of dealing with stress by giving the person a sense of control over his or her life.

Or a family may be overprotective and the children are not allowed to make their own decisions. Teens may feel their weight is something they can be in charge of. People with eating disorders also may come from families where feelings are not discussed openly, and it is considered wrong to express anger or hurt feelings.

Many people with eating disorders have been physically or sexually abused. In this case, the eating disorder can be a cry for help. It can be a way to bury feelings of shame and guilt and to deal with emotional pain. People who are sexually abused grow up with little or no sense of control over their own bodies and their lives. By rigidly controlling their weight, they may be trying to regain a feeling of control over themselves.

Eating disorders will slow, or even prevent, development into adulthood. A girl with an eating disorder stops getting her period, and her breasts and hips shrink. A boy with an eating disorder will stop producing testosterone. This decreases sexual desire and performance. For a girl or boy who has been sexually abused, the developing body may be a reminder of his or her pain and fear. In that case, an eating disorder may express a wish to appear sexually unattractive—to try to stay safe from the abuse, and to avoid sexual attention of any kind. These fears and anxieties are all unconscious. People suffering from eating disorders are not aware that they starve themselves, binge and purge, or exercise compulsively for reasons beyond being thin.

Social Factors

"Everyone always told me how pretty I was and how lucky I was to be thin. I thought my looks must be the best thing I have going for me, so I better make sure I keep them."

"I wanted to be a model. I would look through fashion magazines and think, if I'm going to be a model, this is what I have to look like. And starving myself is the only way I'm going to get there."

We live in a world where people, especially women, are often judged by their appearance. From

Many teens who read fashion magazines can be unaware of the negative effects certain images have on their self-image and self-esteem.

35

Barbie dolls to music videos to fashion models, girls and women are surrounded by unrealistic and unattainable images of the female body. In our society, thin people are thought to be attractive, good, strong, desirable, and successful. Overweight people are often viewed as lazy, socially inept, stupid, undesirable, and lonely. Many experts believe that if there were not such an intense emphasis to be thin and physically fit in our culture, eating disorders would be very rare.

In addition, certain activities, such as modeling, cheerleading, and ballet dancing, emphasize thinness and body shape. So do certain sports,

Many young people who participate in activities and sports that connect weight with performance are particularly vulnerable to the dangers of eating disorders.

such as gymnastics, wrestling, figure skating, swimming, and running. People involved in any of these activities are at higher risk for eating disorders. These days, many coaches and dance instructors are aware of the dangers of eating disorders, and they emphasize the importance of proper nutrition and healthy eating routines. But coaches and teachers who emphasize weight control can encourage eating disorders without realizing it.

Biological Factors

"As far back as I can remember, I would diet whenever I started to have a hard time in school or with a boyfriend. It was the help I could always reach for. It was legal, easy to hide, and cost nothing. The problem was, no one realized it was a drug."

There seems to be a genetic element that makes some people vulnerable to eating disorders. Scientists have found that people with eating disorders may have too much, or too little, of certain hormones. Hormones are chemicals in our bodies that stimulate certain body functions and help keep our minds and bodies running smoothly. No one knows exactly how much of a person's eating disorder is caused by chemical or biological tendencies that he or she was born with. This area is the least understood in relation to eating disorders, but researchers are working to learn more.

Trigger Factors

"My anorexia was under control for a while—until my boyfriend and I broke up. It was the only way I could get through it."

Sometimes an event in someone's life will trigger an eating disorder. A triggering event might be the end of a love relationship. Often it is the beginning of a time of great change, with a new set of expectations, such as graduation, a new school, or a new job. A devastating trauma such as rape, sexual abuse, or incest also can trigger an eating disorder.

Another common triggering factor is weight- or body-related comments from friends, parents, siblings, doctors, or coaches. Young people are very sensitive to what other people think about them, especially people they want to please. Your doctor may say, "You should lose ten pounds." Your coach might joke, "Better lay off the ice cream." But to you it's not funny. You may think, I'm fat! I look terrible! I have to change the way I look! The adult may not realize it, but comments about weight can trigger unhealthy eating and exercise habits, which could develop into an eating disorder.

No Single Cause

Many factors contribute to an eating disorder. The

person who is experiencing it usually does not realize what's going on. It's not as if a person says, "My parents don't pay attention to me, so I'm going to punish them by losing weight." It's an unconscious process, which means it happens without a person's realizing it. Recovering from an eating disorder involves uncovering its causes and learning how to deal with those problems in a healthy way.

How Can Compulsive Exercise Hurt Me?

4

Compulsive exercise, like all eating disorders, damages the body, the mind, and the spirit.

The Physical Price You Pay

"Gradually, I became drained. It would hurt just to walk to class. I was too weak to open a door. I had sores on my legs and arms that would not heal. I was throwing up blood. You know when you work out way

too much, how awful you feel? I felt that way twenty-four hours a day."

"My right shin has all the symptoms of a stress fracture, but I grit my teeth and run anyway. I don't dare say anything, because then I won't be allowed to run. Three weeks ago, when I came back from an early-morning run, I could tell my dad was up because the kitchen light was on. I waited outside until he was out of the room. It was seventeen degrees outside and I was covered in sweat. Now I have a sinus infection that won't go away, but I haven't cut back at all. The strangest thing is that I don't even really like running. But I can't imagine ever stopping, or even cutting back."

The human body needs rest as much as it needs food and water. Even professional athletes do not train every day because they know that they must rest in order to stay strong and fit. Compulsive exercisers don't give their bodies enough time to recuperate. Because of this, they develop painful injuries, such as stress fractures and torn muscles, ligaments, tendons, and cartilage (the soft tissue in the joints).

Food is our body's fuel. The more energy a person expends, the more fuel he or she needs. An athlete needs to eat more than a person who sits at a desk all day. Compulsive exercisers usually do not eat

When the body isn't getting all the nutrients it needs, it shuts down and stops working the way it should.

enough to sustain their high level of activity. Because they use many more calories than they take in, they become very weak and their bodies break down.

All eating disorders cause serious physical problems. People with bulimia develop ulcers (holes or tears) in their stomachs, throats, and mouths, because the gastric (stomach) acid the body uses to digest food is continually brought up through vomiting. Ulcers are very serious and painful and can be fatal. Bulimics often have yellow, damaged teeth. This is also caused by acids brought up into the mouth through repeated vomiting. The acids wear off the protective enamel on the teeth. People with bulimia also get painful stomach cramps from severe constipation. This is caused by the abuse of laxatives, which damages the digestive system. People with bulimia become weak and exhausted.

People with anorexia are always cold. Their hands and feet may look blue. This is because their bodies don't have enough fat to keep them warm. As a result, fine hairs, called lanugo, grow all over their bodies. A girl with anorexia stops producing estrogen (the female hormone), causing her bones to lose mass and weaken. When she gets older, she will be at high risk for osteoporosis. People with anorexia also suffer from painful stomach cramps because the body is physically straining to retain what little nutrition is available. Blood pressure and the heart rate slow down and weaken, so that the whole body is slower and weaker. These effects of starvation can result in death.

Women and girls with eating disorders stop getting their menstrual periods. As a girl recovers, the return of her period is a sign of her returning health.

The Emotional Cost

"I lost all my friends. I had no life, all I had was exercise. I was so unhappy. I thought, Why can't I just eat? Why can't I just be normal? I cried myself to sleep every night."

An eating disorder takes control over a person's life. A person with an eating disorder often feels isolated from family and friends.

"Having an eating disorder isolates you. Meals are a big part of social life. If you can't eat in front of people, you're going to see people less and less."

"I can't remember the last time that I wasn't tired or hurting. I feel so empty all of the time. But if I don't run at the end of a day, I feel even worse. It's like a chance to beat myself up for all the stuff I've screwed up all day. It's a chance to forget everything except how many more miles I have left."

As bad as the physical symptoms are, the emotional toll of an eating disorder can be even worse.

As exercise takes up more and more time, compulsive exercisers become increasingly isolated. That isolation makes them more depressed and unhappy—then they may exercise even more to try to feel better. They have so little contact with other people that their self-image becomes increasingly distorted. They think that anyone who tries to help them is an enemy.

"When people said I was too thin, I thought they were just jealous. When my parents tried to get me to eat, I thought, They can't make me do anything I don't want to do. I'm in complete control here."

"My eating disorder completely took over my life. At its worst, I thought about it every waking moment. I thought I was in control, but it was a trap."

Exercise and diet can provide a temporary escape from stress and give us a feeling of control over our lives. But when diet and exercise become an obsession, they control you. Experts believe that eating disorders are as addictive as cocaine or alcohol. They can be just as dangerous as well.

How to Get Help

Many girls and boys will develop an eating disorder at some point in their lives. It may be in junior high, high school, or in their early twenties.

If you think you may have an eating disorder, chances are that something is bothering you, and it is expressing itself through your eating and exercise habits. You may be comparing your body to others' and feeling that you don't measure up. You may be nervous about the idea of a sexual relationship, feel pressured about your performance in school or sports, or have worries about what life will be like after graduation. These are all very normal concerns—but that doesn't mean they aren't confusing and frightening to you.

Abuse

Unhealthy eating and exercise habits may be related to other traumas in your life, such as abuse. There are three kinds of abuse.

Emotional abuse is when someone continually makes you feel bad about yourself. This can take many forms, such as yelling, name-calling, teasing, cruelty, or constant criticism.

Physical abuse is when someone intentionally causes you physical pain. It includes slapping, hitting, hair-pulling, pushing, shoving, punching, throwing another down or against a wall, burning, or physically hurting someone in any way.

Sexual abuse is being forced to have sexual contact of any kind. Rape is one type of sexual abuse, but force does not have to be physical. If someone threatens to hurt you or someone you love if you don't have sexual activity with them, that is sexual abuse. If an adult family member, friend, or neighbor has sexual activity with a child, it is sexual abuse. The abuser may do something sexual to you or demand that you do something sexual to him.

Either way it is sexual abuse. When you were a child, if a family member, neighbor, teacher, or other adult touched you in a sexual way or made you touch him or her in a sexual way, then you were sexually abused—no matter what they told you.

Many people who have been abused develop eating disorders. Very often, they don't remember the abuse, because their mind represses it. That means the memory is so painful and disturbing that your mind blocks it out. Then the pain expresses itself in other ways. The eating disorder is like the memory coming out. If you have an eating disorder, your body may be trying to tell you something.

Getting Healthy

Some people develop an eating disorder for a short period of time and stop the unhealthy behavior on their own. Many people need counseling to recover from their eating disorders. The chance to talk about what's bothering you and get good nutritional and exercise advice may be enough to get you back on a healthy track.

For many people, an eating disorder becomes a way of life. It is something they feel they cannot live without. If that has happened to you, or you feel it could be happening, it's best to seek help as soon as possible. Speak to a teacher, guidance counselor, school nurse, or someone else you can

Therapy is an important part of eating disorder recovery. Therapy helps people with eating disorders uncover the root of their problems and deal with them in healthier ways.

trust. Your doctor can also recommend a registered dietitian or counselor. Or contact one of the eating disorder organizations listed in the back of this book. They will refer you to someone who can help.

To recover from a serious eating disorder, you will need two things at the same time. You will need nutritional help to rebuild your strength and health. And you will need psychological help to discover the causes of your problem and find healthy ways to deal with your feelings. Many people with serious eating disorders need to spend time in a hospital or treatment facility. In treatment, you work with therapists and nutritionists until you are out of critical danger. After coming out of the program, you continue to see a therapist and nutritionist, usually once or twice each week. There are many treatment facilities to help people with eating disorders. It's important to find the one that's right for you.

"Our group sessions in the treatment center were the first time I had ever opened up to anyone. It was scary, but it felt great! I saw how I hid behind my exercise. I used to think that if you never open up to anyone, you'll never get hurt. But you'll never really live, either."

"The month I spent in treatment was the hardest thing I have ever done in my life. But it was also the greatest thing. It gave me back my life."

Recovering from an eating disorder is like fighting an addiction to drugs or alcohol. It is a long, slow, difficult process, and it may never be 100 percent complete. A recovering alcoholic will always have to be careful—even if he or she hasn't had a drink in years. During periods of stress, he or she may have a strong urge to drink. People with eating disorders will also have ongoing struggles and may relapse many times.

"I was at a healthy weight for almost a year when I found out my boyfriend had been cheating on me. It was too much for me. Before I knew it, I was in the bathroom, throwing up again. The only way I knew how to handle it was by running fifteen miles a day and throwing up. So I went back to therapy."

"I still see my therapist and my nutritionist every week, and I write in my journal every day. I won't lie to you, it's still hard. I have relapses, then I get really mad at myself for that. But I'm dealing with it. Every day I'm alive is another chance to work on it. I'm just glad I got help when I did, or I wouldn't be here now."

Remember, recovery is possible. Many healthy and active people have struggled with an eating disorder at some point in their lives. The important thing is to recognize your problem and get help.

I Have This Friend...

You may have a friend you think is struggling with compulsive exercise, anorexia, or bulimia. How you respond to the problem can make a big difference in the recovery. But remember, you cannot control another person's behavior. You cannot force your friend to exercise less or eat more. You can, however, express your concern and offer your support. Here are some tips for helping.

Try to...

Speak to your friend privately.

Tell your friend you're concerned about her, because you care about her.

Be prepared that she will deny that she has a problem. She may get angry or hostile toward you.

Remember that it's not up to you. You can support and encourage her, but you can't make her recover if she's not ready to.

Try not to...

Speak to anyone else about her before you talk with her. Don't bring a group of friends along to confront her.

Tell her she's doing something "crazy," "sick," or "wrong."

Give her advice about exercise, diet, or her appearance.

Plead, beg, threaten, or get into an argument with her. Try not to get into a power struggle.

Pry or spy. Don't try to be the "Food Police." She'll just resent you and become even more secretive.

Before you speak to your friend, write down the name and phone number or the Internet address of an eating disorder organization. (You'll find some in the back of this book.) After you express your concern and listen to what he or she has to say, offer that phone number. You can try saying, "Why don't you take the number? That way, if you ever want to call, you'll have it." But remember, you can't force your friend to get help. He or she has to want help and be ready to accept it.

In general, it is better to speak directly to your friend before you speak to anyone else about him or her. There is an exception. If you believe your friend is in serious danger, you should tell someone right away. Some signs of danger are: if your friend is throwing up more than once a day, throwing up blood, has a very severe stomachache, or expresses suicidal thoughts. These are emergency situations. Tell an adult whom you trust as soon as possible.

You Are Worth More Than Your Weight

"Now that I've recovered, I see how much time I wasted thinking about my weight, about how much I could exercise, about what I was going to eat. I was missing out on so much life!"

Many people do recover from compulsive exercise and go on to live happy, healthy lives.

"So many girls think if they lost ten pounds, their lives would be so much better. But happiness doesn't come from what you weigh. It comes from who you are, your relationships, what you do with your life. If

your happiness is about how you look, you'll never really be happy."

"I can't believe the things that I did to myself. I never want to do that again. It wasn't living. I had a lot of friends, I was an A student, took dance classes and played piano, but I couldn't enjoy any of it. Now that I'm healthy, this is the first time in my life I feel really good about myself."

Remember:
- If exercise isn't fun or if it makes you feel worse, instead of better;
- If you think about your exercise routine all of the time and always feel that you should be doing more;
- If you keep a list of what you are allowed to eat and only let yourself eat certain amounts of food;
- If you've lost weight, and people tell you you're thin, but you still want to lose more;
- If you think about your body and your weight all of the time;
- If you do things to lose weight that you don't tell anybody about;

then you may have an eating disorder. It can be a serious problem, but it can be overcome.

If someone you care about has an eating disorder, give them this book. If you think you may have a problem, please speak to someone about it. You deserve to get more out of life. You are not what you weigh, and your value as a human being is not reflected in the numbers on a scale.

Glossary

addiction An obsessive/compulsive need for and use of a substance or a behavior.

biological Based in your body, your physical being.

calorie The amount of energy food provides.

compulsive Relating to feeling psychologically unable to resist performing or doing things.

constipation The inability to have a bowel movement, causing cramps, stomachaches, and gas.

discipline Self-control; the ability to stick to a certain routine, behavior, or activity.

distorted Warped; not based in reality.

eating disorder An unhealthy and extreme concern with weight, body size, food, and eating habits.

estrogen Female hormone.

fasting Not eating for a whole day or more.

genetic Relating to the qualities or tendencies that we are born with.

hormones Substances formed in certain glands that control body processes, such as growth.

immune system The body's system for protecting itself from disease and infection.

laxative A pill or liquid that brings on a bowel movement.

metabolism The processes by which the body turns food into energy.

nutrition What and how we eat to nourish and maintain a healthy body.

perfectionist Someone who is never satisfied with his or her own performance, appearance, grades, or other achievements; someone who believes that anything less than perfection is failure.

psychological Having to do with the inner workings of the mind; mental.

purge To get rid of food suddenly and harshly, usually by vomiting, exercise, or laxatives.

self-esteem Confidence, self-respect, satisfaction with oneself.

self-image How a person sees and thinks of herself or himself.

testosterone Male hormone.

trauma An event in a person's life that is highly disruptive, very negative, and life-changing.

Where to Go for Help

American Anorexia/Bulimia Association (AABA)
165 West 46th Street, Suite 1108
New York, NY 10036
(212) 575-6200
Web site: http://members.aol.com/AMANBU

Anorexia Nervosa and Related Eating Disorders, Inc. (ANRED)
P.O. Box 5102
Eugene, OR 97405
(541) 344-1144
Web site: http://www.anred.com

Eating Disorders Awareness and Prevention, Inc. (EDAP)
603 Stewart Street, Suite 803
Seattle, WA 98101
(206) 382-3587
Web site: http://members.aol.com/edapinc

National Association of Anorexia Nervosa and Associated Disorders (ANAD)
Box 7
Highland Park, IL 60035
(847) 831-3438
Web site: http://members.aol.com/anad20/index.html

National Eating Disorders Organization (NEDO)
6655 South Yale Avenue
Tulsa, OK 74136
(918) 481-4044
Web site: http://www.laureate.com

In Canada

Anorexia Nervosa and Associated Disorders (ANAD)
109-2040 West 12th Avenue
Vancouver, BC V6J 2G2
(604) 739-2070

The National Eating Disorder Information Centre
College Wing, 1st Floor, Room 211
200 Elizabeth Street
Toronto, ON M5G 2C4
(416) 340-4156

For Further Reading

Berry, Joy. *Good Answers to Tough Questions About Weight Problems and Eating Disorders*. Chicago: Children's Press, 1991.

Clark, Nancy. *Nancy Clark's Sports Nutrition Guidebook*, 2nd ed. Champaign, IL: Human Kinetics, 1996.

Cooke, Kaz. *Real Gorgeous: The Truth About Body and Beauty*. New York: W. W. Norton, 1996.

Crook, Marion. *Looking Good: Teenagers and Eating Disorders*. Toronto: NC Press, Ltd., 1992.

Folkers, Gladys, and Jeanne Engelman. *Taking Charge of My Mind and Body: A Girls' Guide to Outsmarting Alcohol, Drugs, Smoking, and Eating Problems*. Minneapolis: Free Spirit Publishing, 1997.

Kano, Susan. *Making Peace with Food*. New York: HarperCollins, 1989.

Kolodny, Nancy J. *When Food's a Foe: How You Can Confront and Conquer Your Eating Disorder*. New York: Little, Brown and Company, 1992.

Siegel, Michele, Judith Brisman, and Margot

Weinshel. *Surviving an Eating Disorder: New Perspectives and Strategies for Family and Friends.* New York: HarperCollins, 1997.

Gürze Books is a publisher that specializes in books on eating disorders. The following books, as well as many others, can be ordered directly from them. The books will be sent to you in a plain, confidential package.

Gürze Books
P.O. Box 2238
Carlsbad, CA 92018
(800) 756-7533

Cohen, Mary Anne. *French Toast for Breakfast: Declaring Peace with Emotional Eating.*
Hall, Lindsey. *Full Lives: Women Who Have Freed Themselves from Food and Weight Obsession.*
        . Bulimia: A Guide to Recovery.
Zerbe, Kathryn. *The Body Betrayed: A Deeper Understanding of Women, Eating Disorders, and Treatment.*

Index

About the Author

Laura Kaminker has been a freelance writer for thirteen years. She has written books, magazine articles, and educational videos and has worked with teenagers as a teacher and a counselor. An article she wrote about compulsive exercise appeared in *Seventeen* magazine. She lives in New York City with her partner, Allan Wood, and their two dogs.

Design and Layout: Christine Innamorato

Consulting Editor: Michele I. Drohan

Photo Credits

Photo on p. 9 © Giovanni Lunardi/International Stock; p. 12 © Barry Rosenthal/FPG International; p. 14 © Steven Jones/FPG International; p. 16 by Ira Fox; pp. 22, 40, 46 © Skjold Photographs; p. 24 © Brian Drake/ Viesti Associates, Inc.; p. 27 by Maike Schulz; pp. 30, 33 by Pablo Maldonado; pp. 33, 49 by Seth Dinnerman; pp. 35, 44 by Les Mills; p. 36 © Dusty Willison/International Stock; p. 42 by John Bentham; p. 54 © Mark Scott/FPG International.